LUM

LOVE SONGS

TO

CARIBBEAN AMERICAN LIFE

FAITH P. NELSON

Luminescent Ships: Love Songs to Caribbean American Life

Published by Watercourse LLC

Copyright © September 2023 by Faith P. Nelson All rights reserved. No part of this book may be reproduced, stored, transmitted or circulated in any form without the prior consent of the author or publisher.

Made in the USA

Book Cover Design: Assembled in Canva
Cover Art: Lauretta Jo McCoy
www.laurettajmccoy.com
Interior Illustrations: Canva

"Elegy for Andrea Johnson Ocran" published with permission.

ISBN: 978-0-9975917-4-3

Other Poetry by Faith P. Nelson

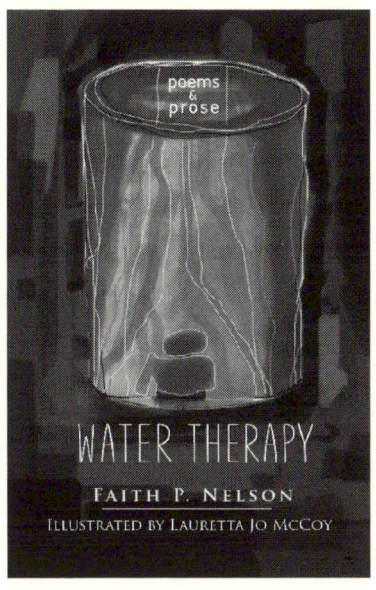

Table of Contents

Introduction	1
Marcus Garvey Sighting	3
Caribbean Origin Story	6
Sometimish Stepmother Villanelle	9
Somebody Will Come	11
The Iron On Mi So Bazodee	14
How Was It, Claude?	16
Caricom Cuisine	20
Near Howard University	23
Bony Imperialism	25
The Foster Girls	28
New Arrival	31
Questions After A Funeral	33
Luminescent Ships	37
Tilley Lamp Bedtime Rhyme	41
Games We Dared Not Play With Our Grandmothers	44
Would Be Alright With Some Florida Soil	48
Sunday Prep	51
Pet Conversations	54

Determination	57
Two Cities	59
Nation Sounds	61
Black Shine	64
Immigrant Family Duppies	66
Dancehall's Unlikely Feminist	69
Affirm	72
Strange Love on Georgia Avenue	74
Notes	77
Acknowledgements	79
About the Poet	80

Introduction

I wanted to write a series of lighthearted quatrains about Caribbean American life in the USA. No quatrains appeared. Other forms of poetry did. So did Marcus Garvey, a lot. I let it be. Some poems focus on our indelible contributions to this society. Others focus on a memory, the quick flashes of home.

Artist Lauretta McCoy created the cover art for this chapbook. Knowing of her highly poetic approach to painting and layering images and symbols, I sent her three of the poems and asked if she would consider doing the art.

I noticed another piece of synchronicity. Lauretta had provided a written piece for an African diaspora anthology by another author. The submission was her grandmother's fragment of memory about Marcus Garvey, whom I honor in this chapbook.

We are communicating on so many levels. Poetry and art are bridges between. It was a piece of art, a symbol that recovered Lauretta's grandmother's memory of Garvey. That memory lights our imagination about a moment in Garvey's life, how he may have navigated the American South.

With permission, I have included Lauretta's contribution about Marcus Garvey in this book. It makes sense. I hope this small collection does the same thing as art: help re-knit the fabric of memory of Caribbean American life.

Marcus Garvey Sighting

My maternal grandmother Laura Felton Crockett grew up in Winston-Salem, North Carolina. We called her Mamma Crockett. My mother sent my sisters and I to visit her every summer to get us out of the city. As soon as we got to Mamma Crockett, we would start updating her about the day-to-day happenings in Washington, DC—the slangs, the new styles, music and such. When I was fourteen, I wore a denim jacket full of sewn-on patches to her house. That was the latest style—peace signs, flowers and black pride symbols. They were very popular amongst the African American youth during that time.

We were in the kitchen moving around and I happened to turn my back to her. She noticed the big red, black and green patch covering the back of my jacket and was very surprised by it. She said it looked familiar to her. I was so excited to tell Mamma Crockett that this was the African Liberation Flag created by Marcus Garvey. Red is for the blood, black is for the people and green is for the land.

She then recalled that when she was a young girl, a gentleman named Marcus Garvey stayed at the boarding house owned by her father, Joseph Clinton Felton. She was born in 1906 and would have been in her teens when she met him. I couldn't believe my ears. Marcus Garvey, my hero, had stayed at my great grandfather's boarding house. Papa Felton was a salesman and built himself a fine stone house in which he took in boarders all the time. The boarding house was so important for people of color during the Jim Crow era that there is now a proposal in place to acknowledge it as a Green Book site.

Mamma Crockett said that Marcus Garvey was in that area because he was going to a rally. He asked her if she would sew a flag for him and she did in those very colors she remembered—red, black, and green.

Lauretta McCoy
Artist, Illustrator, and Creative Director

Caribbean Origin Story

The One. The Word. Supreme. All-seeing
To be clear, Him substitute for Big G.
So I can get on with this storytelling
How God use a broom to sweep back the sea
Him gouge a shape, a cosmic banana bunch
Then him summon him trainees, him have a lot
And him give them three of his smaller words.
Make an eye. Him point him chin to mark the spot
Him waving hand make a ridge, true true wud
An eyebrow squinting in almond-shaped delight
Laugh lines crackle, make a brow. If you see mud!
Trainees play: ripple-ping-ripple-pung-pie
Each tune on their kora pop up an island
There the Caribbean. If you see sand!

Then god pull a golden string from him heart
If you see dazzling light. You think is lie.
Millions of almond-shaped flying sparks
Some turn into flowers, hummingbirds, flies
Green algae, future human healing guide
Some seeds wanted to thank the wellspring
We want to clap our hands, they cried.
And Source chin-pointed to the makers in training
And they trust one hundred and sounded the kora
Rich ochre limbs formed, same ones we using now

Then Big G burn out the memories of the future
If you fear too much, you will distrust the very cow
Anyway, is the All-giving so Him let the water in
A living cup full almost to the brim.

Sometimish Stepmother Villanelle

June is the month we celebrating wi mother
the sun girl with a baby polymath on her teat.
Stepmother watches from Love Isle with a glower.

Give me the wretched refuse from your teeming shoulder
Due respect Ma'am. Me is mi own woman, yuh seeit.
June is the month we celebrating wi mother.

The I-man is a cold-tolerant traveler, a reggae doctor
a conscious weed seed. Is nature do it.
Stepmother watches from Love Isle with a glower.

We and the Lenape, foundation provider
scientists, artists, renaissance fleet
June is the month we acknowledging wi mother.

Tallawah, we de present and we designing the future
We invent and pull together. We transform and defeat
and we schooling stepmother about the full culture.

Let me hear you say woh-oh-oh, psalm singer
Chant away the fever blister, the cultural deceit
June is the month we celebrating wi mother.
Stepmother, she can stay on Love Isle and glower.

Somebody Will Come
(For Marcus Mosiah Garvey)

jettisoned, we bob
on a grim sea clutching life
somebody will come

teeth beating morse code
send a David or a John
somebody must come

fingers fork and rake
in thrall of cotton and cane
somebody must see

human coral bleed
we making bank for the west
somebody witness

oy you rise up nuh
the voice hammers and chisels
sound digging up we

purple golden, with
mouth made of tightly coiled words
my kingfisher bird

ole time hat with plume
a sight for watering eyes
this man sunning we

praise to the most high
break my fear's bones, crack this load
with love's medicine.

(First published August 17, 2022)

The Iron On Mi So Bazodee

The iron dance down the road
on the multicolored float. It beats
launching rings of power through the air
catching two, three notes per second
to shower dancers' ears
we catch some with our feet
our two halves surprised at each other
the fast scissoring of a football player
feint this way, dribble, cut to the goal
jump to the unrelenting beat.
The unwinding must never stop
every sweep of our hips and hands
trace the curves of sacred geometry
June is for what makes the bridge
between our two selves
we get drunk on the joining.

How Was It, Claude?

1.

Claude sends a piece of himself
beaming down on Utica Avenue
in Brooklyn, curious to feel the changes.
His ported self thrills as he walks
into the oncoming crowd, brushing
shoulders clad in high and low styles
faces of all hues some sullen, bopping
humming, toasting, hands and fingers
bladed, chopping air. Where was the music?
No more three-piece wool suits
toe tags signaling trustworthiness.
No blacks stepping off the sidewalk.

2.

Dinner in a modern Caribbean eatery.
Tuning in like an obeah man to the past
year's happenings. Carnival truck DJs
screaming over three four stanzas worth
the madness a geyser through surprised
vocal cords and a wide open mouth.
Jamaicans call it bawling out
Urban songs on the flatbed truck mask
prayers in the West African wilderness
the roars of our endangered inner lions

so long after the renaissance. *Ah, Marcus
You were right. Back to Africa was a proper
rallying cry, a vent. But what now?*

3.

Watching the street through the window
he bites the last of his grilled snapper sandwich
and licks his invisible sauce-coated fingers
"Claude McKay," says a hoarse squeak.
"We were just talking about you!"
Claude stares up at the young black fellow
with a brown satchel hugging his chest and hip.
Then his brown eyes scan the loud room.
Nobody else seemed interested.
The young man popped out a small tablet
A fragment of his poem appeared
"then even the monsters we defy ..."
Backside! Some people can see me dung here.
"I'm a ... we are poets," the fellow stammered
He turned and waved urgently. Chair legs
scraped. Five more young people.
They crowded into the window seat next to him
Backside. Some people can see me dung here.

4.

His bigger self welcomes him back
Inside the gleaming ship arms wide

He's a parent pleased as pus.
I see that yuh had fun.
How yuh feeling, was it worth it?
Well ... inspiration you know.
I want to write poetry again so
yes I had to goh back to where
it all began. Dis time I'm exploring
in the vernacular. Yuh know seh I run into
some young poets who could see me?
Nearly spit out mi fish sangwidge
inna dem face, mi so shock. Yeah man
the fight still a gwan dung deh
but there is hope—
The voice thins out as the two selves
merge and walk towards the bridge.

Caricom Cuisine

seasonings different
but now we experience
all islands cuisine

doubles and jerk shrimp
washed down with ginger sorrel
wid a side of bunji

coconut plus rice
red peas soaked all night, garlic
smell the pimento

yam, shredded roti
saltfish, ackee and pear. bus
up shut and belly

stinking toe fruit sweet
thick peach milkshake on a seed
horlicks birth mother

caribbean mail
indian spice rides trade winds
saffron powdered love

pudding: hell a top
me in the middle mouth open
bliss in me wiyah

bitter orange fruit
lemonade with character
this rind is true life

you see banana
the west indian one dem
sweet pineapple taste

foreign dessert dream
julie mango ice-cream kotch
pon top drunk black cake

Near Howard University

old howard parties
dollar wine, steam from corn soup
police sirens rise

drum and bass pulsing
we don't care bout the mean chef
curry goat ration

dub was a deep thrill
no cross-eyed parents watching
your figure eight wine

soca, reggae, zouk
dancing in big shoes, tracing
stokely carmichael

but what a kingdom
thurgood, kamala harris
walking the same quad

house party las lick
carolina, like clockwork
police returning

howard party done
no no we ain't going home
we crowdin ihop

Bony Imperialism

social media chef prevail
substitute turkey neck for dear oxtail
yes, break out the we-shall-overcome
boycott cowtail imperialism

why the Caribbean buy so much fossil
fuel that make the sky co2 awful
break out the we-shall-overcome
boycott cowtail imperialism

why we not trapping more electrons
from the equatorial west indian sun
break out the we-shall-overcome
boycott cowtail imperialism

why the Caribbean in ganja purgatory
it's gold for Colorado's economy
break out the we-shall-overcome
boycott cowtail imperialism

why Caribbeans import billions in food
islands, grow some of that! be shrewd
break out the we-shall-overcome
boycott cowtail imperialism

why some Caribbeans disparage patois
english came from an old norse grandpa
break out the we-shall-overcome
boycott cowtail imperialism

why oxtail fifteen dollars a pound
everybody ask the butcher with a frown
break out the we-shall-overcome
boycott cowtail imperialism.

The Foster Girls

something about these sisters
second generation cradle
of Caribbean American life
four female voices
in a brightly colored butterfly opera
presented at dinner time
young sopranos circling
practicing their reasoning
against their father's Jamaican bass
branches on a mahogany tree
weaving new life.

they are close in age. when they talk
they battle not to win but to test
and strengthen
to make a strong argument
confidently write their stories
build future leaders, warrior women
but daddy the reason for your objection
can't be just because I said so
starkly different from our own experience
sax and guitar in a reggae band
no less than the king drum and bass
carving out their own solos
up and down they go imitating
the green backbone of our island past.

often they whisper
their made-up language mumbling
dem laugh till dem dead
the sound echoing throughout
each sister starting again as soon as breath
when one imitates their father's sound
framing a moment, dramatizing ...
capturing his foreign accent
mouth movements and gesticulations
his patois rebuke to a second gen request.

relaxed chief audience
he takes in their antics
their copied Jamaican accents
their soon-to-be borrowed Jamaican values
and he chuckles, recognizing their pouring love.

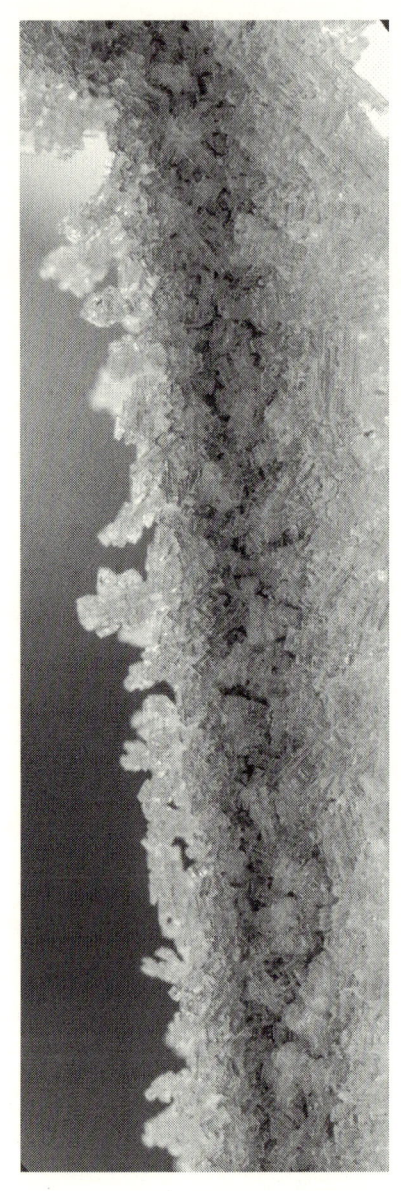

New Arrival

For long moments my teeth grind
into the memory of old mango trees
crowding their branches
battling the sun for my love.
It's not worth it, I jiggle my muscles
my shoulders grab the thin coat.
It was 3:00 o'clock and bright.
At the naked bus stop I peered north
for the oblong gray head of the S2.

Friends, well-seasoned turkey
Now in a well-sugared stupor
on America's most loving holiday
I whispered a prayer for my forgotten
gloves, the full-bodied yet silky
red-peas rice and peas cooked with
imported coconuts, for what Miss Lou
calls colonization in reverse, the bus
the driver, the chef, my returning
memory, a little bit of humility
the first people, African hands—

The souls up there working
sat back in their rocking chairs
some laying down their quilting
It's all a game, that's all it is
they said. First Thanksgiving prayer.

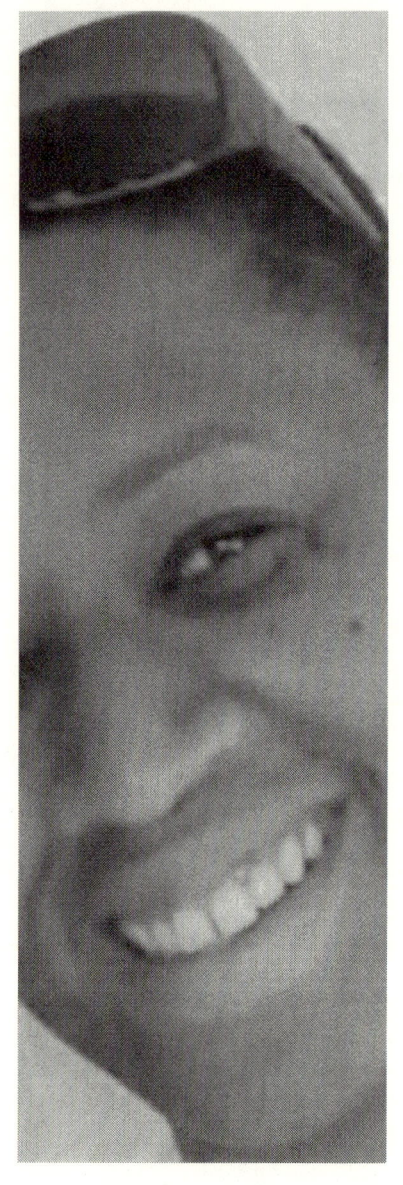

Questions After A Funeral
(Elegy For Andrea Johnson Ocran)

I stare at your skin for a long time
waiting for flow, for the light to return
to your steel pan playing hands
but you are a step ahead, shedding
the physical, keeping the experience
diving into bottomless love for family.
Is it like when you taught me to drive
a stick shift car balancing easing easy
gas foot up clutch foot down braking
then parking for the heroic return?

Where are you now so-young Andrea
petals and muscles no longer tired
Shelley-Ann after pounding the track
ready for your next assignment
proud of the rigor of life schooling
sailing freely through the cosmos
your A+ debriefing wrapped.
are you within earshot
of your loved ones. Ready to answer:
Mom, which cleats have the magic
      which club should I give my tick
Mom, I got 50 kills today!
      I know you were watching me play
Mom, how to make stew peas taste Jamaican
Are you tapping the keyboard, saying
mm-hmmm to your brother all day

might as well be in the same office
are you nodding with your heart
easing your hubby's mourning?

What did you see with your body Andrea
bionic soul eyes spying up and down
discerning chaff between a person's words
like a farmer tending crops, ripping
away yellowed leaves when they refused
the blood from the earth, the sun
Getting to the heart of the matter
They suck the plant of energy
You sure saw the value of time
efficient one. Are you talking
to your mom now comparing notes
between chuckles. Afrobeats
and reggae pulsing
double tenor steel pan pealing?

I dreamed of you walking in high heels
crisp clunks visiting the wooden floor
the sound growing muscular.
Did you drop by to tell us secrets
of the magnitude of the other side. No?
Only, gone is not really gone. Thrive.
Connect like river loving stone.
Outside on the cul-de-sac turned
soccer field, Ocrans run jostle
listening for you as they kick
the soccer ball and score their goal.

Black jerseys seam with the dusky air
loving your connection like river to stone.
Did you urge them, *please go out and play*?

Luminescent Ships

Poet Bea Veitch Clennon beams
about her dad Dr. Felix Gordon Veitch
graduate of Meharry Medical, Fisk
first speaker of the House Jamaica.
She still stoosh Caribbean after entrees
using polished dessert forks, ironed linen
serviettes beside bone thin cake plates.
Her poems are the pièce de résistance
words about soul's journey and love
we are Source's luminescent ships.

Noel Dexter
Caribbean ethnomusicologist
coaxing traditional and worship music
from north Bahamas to south Aruba.
Red mahogany floors reflect
multiplying sunlight and tapping shoes
curtains dance in the soft breeze
blue mountains Sunday party
the piano thrills at the attention
him playing folk in the high house.

Black Latinos
visiting from Bluefields
buzzing after successful meetings
at the world's iron-tough banks.
No question Nicaraguan-Jamaican history
Eeehms, ehmmms and ee-hihs sandwiched
between Spanish palabras about development
negotiating for the diaspora
language is a smelter's pot
burning assumptions from our brains.

Uncle Leo Edwards
statesman on the front line
flag bearing on Channel 4, 7 and 9
marches with Transafrica's Randall.
Swelling with warrior spirits who have come
a multitude locks arms for South Africa
branding Massachussetts Avenue
chanting to banish apartheid
black people's freedom song
we in the middle of everything.

The Hon. Shirley Nathan Pulliam
state senator of Maryland
but first the years showing up
ten deep with praise for the diaspora.
Every embassy, every event
Shirley yuh no tired! Back
next day the hub and spokes
using her body, throwing her light
to build audience and interest
medals for more than bills passed.

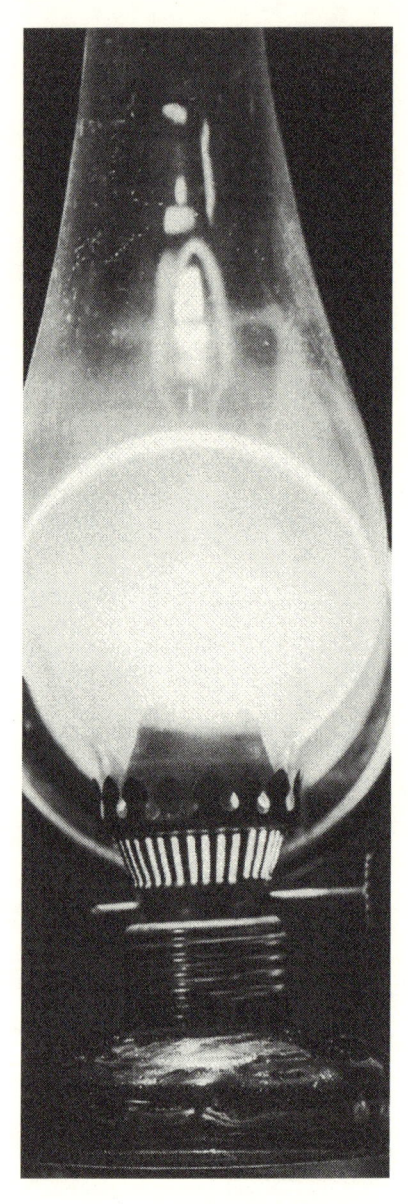

Tilley Lamp Bedtime Rhyme

Goodnight dead of night country dark
thick as thieves with the rolling calf
running with the big chain clanking
dem foul breath singing and panting
please dear God my soul to keep
Mek him pass me over so me get some sleep.

Goodnight croaking lizards, yuh too brazen
demon assistant to Wes Craven
don't even run when fire blazing
if you drop on mi head, yuh bore right in
mi seh mi prayers and twist in the sheet
mi fight and fight, so mi noh drop asleep.

Goodnight scorpions full of malice
slip in wi pajamas wid yuh hungry chalice
wait for stupid we to plant wi leg in
instead of giving the pants a good beating
We hear the laughter but we can't see it
then boom, the venom. Yuh done wi sleep.

Goodnight drummer cockroach, flat brown bird
why you haffi travel in such a big herd
not even car can crush yuh, pestilence king
find a hole in wi house, invite yuhself in
Then you fly straight at wi shuddering heap
Seeit deh now! A how we a go sleep.

Goodnight home-sweet-home in the hurricane
Your torch beats back the rough and the rain
faithful kerosene lamp glowing
your yellow flame heart jus a winking
warning the duppy: don't be a creep
shining your light so we get good sleep.

Games We Dared Not Play With Our Grandmothers

Children Children
Yes Mummah

Where have yuh been to
Gran Mummah

What did she give yuh
Bread and pear

Where's my share
Up in the air

How can I reach it
Climb on a broken chair

Suppose I fall
I do not care

Oooo learn you dat manners
The dog

Oooo is the dog
You!

Wi laugh till wi belly hurt wi
hands on knees only for a moment.
Our spindly legs pump as we run
flit like the doctor bird to invisible buds.
From behind yellow and green croton

bushes, a little bit of worn red cloth
peeps out. Finding me is no challenge.

Dandy shandy. Bet yuh cyan lik me.
The As sound long, the Ns a trampoline
the first syllables homing in on the sing-song
iambic rhythm sprouting between our
shoulder blades rolling up and down
around our thin hips like hula hoops.
We leap over the ball, run, fall
bounding up before the ball hits us
slide, not caring about rough gravel
piercing young skin. Gweh bwoy!
Granny bristles at the brawling behavior.
Akimbo, we fling bony bodies
left and right and round and round
sliding the play words free.

Thin high voices float over the valley
Mek we go to the tamarind treeeeeee.
Time to dust off the crisp brown shells
and crack them with our teeth
snaking out the pulpy sweet and sour fruit
We coat them with sugar pinched
from our grandmother's kitchen. Loving
the feast, our mouths spurt juice and praise.
our lips shoot with the shiny black seeds

Light from the Saturday sun, pierce
the treetops landing on the husked shells
and our eyes. Soul says thanks for the fun.

Would Be Alright With Some Florida Soil

While in dappled villages sitting on parents' hips
leaning back to counter the steep slant of hillsides
we learned horticulture and eating in the wild.
This rough grainy brown oval is a naseberry
inside a sweet pale orange custard bomb.
This scalloped brown pod is tamarind
sweet and sour candy, for tongue-clapping
This bamboo stalk is the epic sugar cane
peeling it makes your teeth last your whole life.
This heart-shaped fruit is mango, filling
buttery, sweet lunch for the whole nation.
This vine is cerasse, bitter medicine
to deworm after a summer of foraging.

Too far away to run through the mango grove
coat our childhood legs and feet with fine red dust
target the break point, the most giving part of the stem
stone down ripe East Indians or common varieties
rub the fruit on our clothes and bite into the thin skin
vacuum the yellow flesh with our hunger
scrape the seed white with our incisors
repeat the pleasurable action ten more times
plaster our lower face skin with the thick jam
clean our jaws and lips with our tongue on the way.

Restive under a mid-atlantic oak, I hear chuckles
Caribbean-American farmers like Ananci whisper

*Me come yah fi drink milk, me noh come yah
fi count cow.* I straighten my back, cock my ears
envious yet admiring this green magic. From Florida
a friend Jen called. *Guess what we picked today.
Ackees.* The wonder sounded in the upper
notes of her voice wrapping thrilled laughter
We both acknowledge this sleight of hand. Before
that she had an expanse of green, only for viewing
a summer golf course for dragonflies and cardinals.
I stare at the oak treetop and the one next to it
a little glum that the acorn is not of my childhood.
Thank God Florida soil will hold some of the seeds
celebrating the wild of our Caribbean homeland.

Sunday Prep

Sidling between shoppers and cartons
of ackee. *Excuse mi.* You pick a number
Excuse, excuse mi, you say to someone.
It turns into *beg pardon* to the bulk
under your foot and the umbrage
on his face. *Is your toe that?* You
apologize with slack jaw and eyes
not even you can believe this craziness.
Number sixty-seven, sixty-seven.

Me, you say to the five butchers
for one shop. *Thank God shopkeeper
travel with dem culture. Five pounds
of chicken feet please.* That is
forty-five feet times four toes.
So much clipping with the kitchen scissors.
It's not Castries, Coronation or Chaguanas market
but look, thank God you have shelter.

How thick do you want the oxtail?
The butcher holds up two finger joints
an emphatic shake of the head
deciding not to compete with the whine
of the meat saw. *One please
Too many people for dinner.*

You and David Rudder make you way
through the aisles peering at every label.

Pim pi lim pim baye lay
somebody lifts a piece of yellow yam
as heavy as the bass pan
lips moving. Your green chochos
move through the air like shekeres
they land in your hand with a drum slap.

Not a walk to the plantain bin
but a Bele from Martinique.
You run eyes
over the cart as you hum.
The whole shop chorusing again
Pim bi lim bim baye biddy bamba
you do a Dinki Mini folk step
because is not Trinidad you grow
Pim pi lim pim baye lay.

The cash register like a non-stop train.
Keep your eye on the counting as you
sing *This girl from Bahia* one last time.
Spending money pleasant sometimes.
Soca in she samba, samba in she soca.

Sunday dinner set.

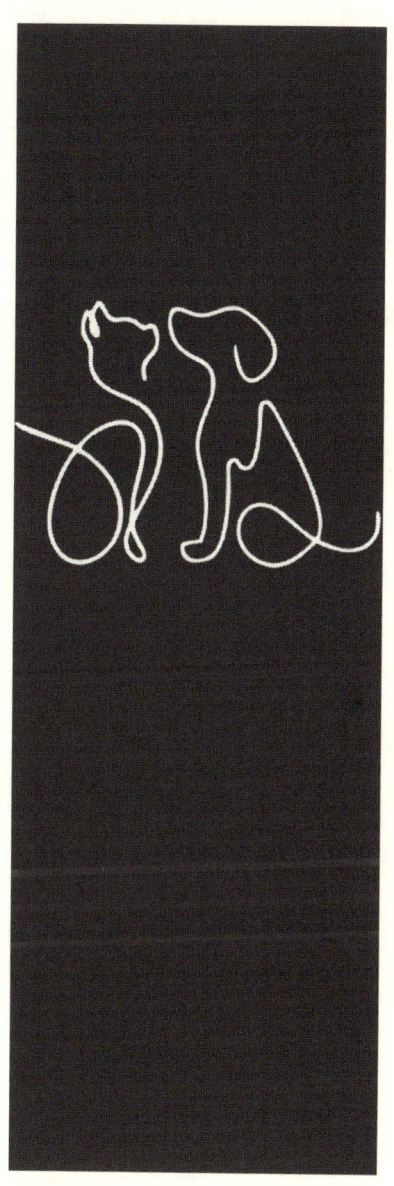

Pet Conversations

My friend Mark has a dog.
His name is Rudy
like the one in Marley's Let Him Go
that 1966 rock steady song.
Jimmy Cliff was a Rudy too
The Harder They Come
This terrier collie Rudy doesn't have gun
But he can get in that crouch like Jimmy does
drop that leash and watch him run
up the blacktop and the grassy hill.

I got a shorthair cat.
His name is Bear
ignored me when I toured the pound
On his first day home he looked around
All the rats in the community
watched themselves after him come.
Matthew Henson in the arctic
I would be bereft without this explorer
conquering the cold of every heart
blonde tabby soul excavator.

Two Caribbean-American houses
both pets smell curry chicken
and ask why they can't get some
West Indian pets eat like humans

their long life and health unaffected
by hot pepper jerk chicken mixed
with cook-up rice and ground provision
You say: Hi Rudie Baby
play panting start, wheeling and dashing.
You say: Bear, be quiet
His jaw becomes a hinge, more argument
You tell them three four times sit down
The fifth time you tell them
Mi seh you fi siddung
They understand
animal souls, living
Caribbean American life.

Determination

Ready for the journey
a refugee on a marathon
from stunted growth, hunger's radiation.
Answers the call of soul
the hero struck by light
Garvey before his American Iration.
She asks for a fifth of water
at the US-Mexico border
and challenges refugee-American relations.
Come death or holiday laughter
come visa, come enforcer
border boss, time for self-determination.
We all going to hear the same song
why should I fall asleep, postpone
bursting the pupa for this actuation.
The soft voice sings, come
in my thick sturdy ears
why ignore this divine suggestion.
It shouldn't matter my sport
that my medals will or won't be
it matters that I accept the invitation.

Two Cities

Big grey buildings rise from black geometric
rivers full of goldfish darting to and fro
nature paints the city with pigeons
hugging the parapets of the jeweled chrysler
digging claws into frozen eagles and gargoyles
dodging mind-your-own-business faces
playing hopscotch with chewing gum
farms in christian louboutin shoes
spit and poop no matter the money
new direction to go.
Harlem way
The flash of black, gold, and green
another sighting of Marcus Garvey.

Softer space wrapping stone monuments
stretching for 68 square miles or so
a satin white dome dotted with square light
houses—535 ringside stadium seats
low-slung savannah with white ant hills
gnawing at itself from the inside
chocolate city tours
the city-wide museum
look at us, beautiful living art.
Independence Avenue
A flash of black me
occasional student of Marcus Garvey.

Nation Sounds

Noise ordinance always—

In the DC region business machines
and sirens, king sounds trundle
on the main street running
by my apartment
the rough growl of trash trucks
diesel straining to make it up
the flat road, to haul away evidence.
Occasionally helicopters chop
their way northeast to southwest
towards Georgetown?
The train with Tropicana cars
rumbles sedately through our town
forced air announces itself
every thirty minutes yet
very few dogs bark knowing
noise ordinances have been passed.
Voices keep themselves inside
their bony soundproofed bodies
I close the soundproofed door
so I can hear the poem.

Bangarang sometimes—

On the island, the machinery of art
intervene, big boxes love dancehall

and soca, big bass wraps your body
a masseuse pounding away clotted
questions about food and money.
Below the hills early night, the treble
preachers, quarrels, tree frogs, crickets
and lovers' voices ride the warm air
rising action in this universal story.

And still the island sleeps
along the coastline the water swells
trillions of drops dash against sand and rock
dragging our thundering worries out to sea
refreshing teachers, government's workers
higglers and the tourists that keep going.

Black Shine

Coal came first
since you are appropriating
for your earlobes and dem pointing fingers

Shine bright
The black the foundation of things
The black who said let freedom ring

Coal came first
since you are stealing
us for your tobacco and your cotton

Coal came first
Marcus says, think glorious
Black skin is not a badge of shame

Coal came first
since you keep killing our stories, forgetting
the money you owe us mobster

Shine bright like venus in the morning
the black titrated from the African
the black who worked this new land

Coal came first
since you are pretending
you don't know where diamonds come from.

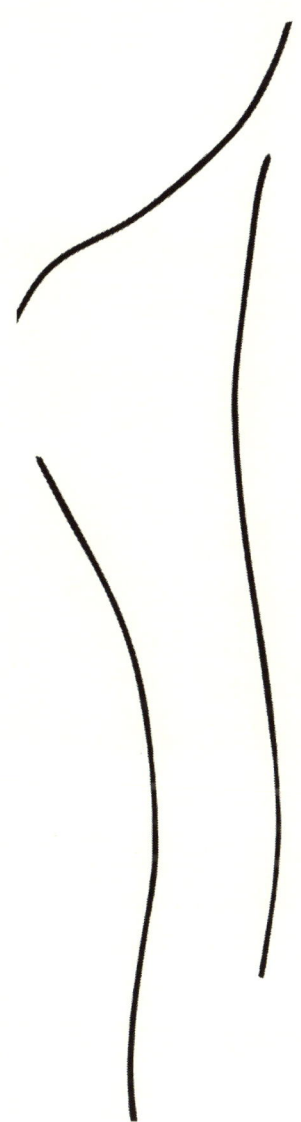

Immigrant Family Duppies

If you decide your sixth sight
is the soft yard clothes you leave behind
be honest while you are packing

Tell dead grandmother Lucille you are going
far away and will see her on your return

Else, your Grandmother can wraith
herself and fly beside your plane

Becoming clouds when she's bored
follow you across the vast ocean

Free to come and go where she pleases
you will see her in your new kitchen

If food was your thing back when, you smell
her safe bosom or her fried dumplings and sprat

Unimpressed with foreign social conventions
she will sing beside you in the subway

Her body will form planetary space
between you and unzipped creeps

Unraveling the how of inner life is a waste
just know Caribbean duppies love to travel

Both of you slide through doors
experiencing plane after plane

You will be spiritual pilgrims praying
in monasteries and crowded markets

If you decide not to take sixth sight
then seeing is hallucinating
the soft yard clothes you leave behind.

Dancehall's Unlikely Feminist

Arleen a mussi dream yuh deh dream
Send her in mi house fi go cook and clean
when me tek a stock she ah read magazine
Arleen a mussi dream yuh deh dream.

Nineteen eighty was a fiery year
political war with new killing gear
blood baths for sale to finance election
worthy causes suffer from lack of attention
rice and peas and chicken give way
to gas belching and bangbelly tension
women's rights haffi tun han mek fashion
And then an unlikely messenger.

But how girl power can sneaky soh
Look how it use General Echo
Iconic stalag riddim broadcasting misogyny
But check how many men talk with authority
Bout Arleen and her brand of insurgency
Now all girls know about this fraternity
Beat box it wid mi: boom-boom
Boo-doo-boo-dum, chiki-boom-boom
Chalkboard in a dancehall schoolroom
As far away as Washington DC/New York, Echo
Toasts from Bobby Newby's music machine
Arleen a mussi dream yuh deh dream
Send her in mi house fi go cook and clean

When me tek a stock she ah read magazine
Arleen a mussi dream yuh deh dream.

Wisdom ride music like a shape shifter
A dancehall hypnotist, a weight lifter
Showing us a galaxy of possibilities
Showing that girl could be a co-ruler.

We nuh come yah fi drop dead a cooking station
Noh tek wi fi granted. Dis a evolution.

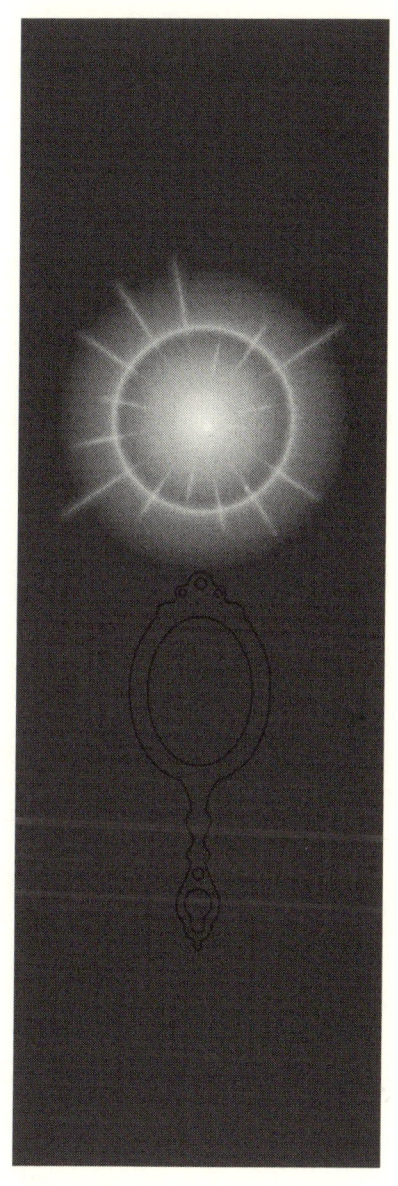

Affirm

We born wid millions of wings, mek dem rise
Breathe deep, fluff dem up mek dem fly
Weh di love weh you say you a go bring
Dis love that come from within
Look pon you beauty inna de mirror
Connect wid the true self, that know everything
Tina Turner get calm with a Buddhist chant
Don't Worry, Marley's anti—depressant
You nah come buy out my head space man
One love up miself, serious ting
Check de bad talk at de door
Dismiss dem, you inner self you must adore
-Your life is more than the blues
-Tek yuh heart outa laced up shoes
We born wid millions of wings mek dem rise
breathe deep, fluff dem up make dem fly.

Strange Love on Georgia Avenue

Just before Christmas, June walked into Blue Nile on Georgia Avenue. She was brewing ginger sorrel for Christmas dinner.

"Hey Kwasi. How tings going!" She hailed the shop owner as she walked to the shelves.

She bent at the waist. Her slightly disembodied voice filled the top of her head as she read the labels.

"Did the black cohosh come in, Kwasi? I have been waiting for it for months. What is going on?"

She straightened up and walked toward another section of the shelves. She grabbed the bottle of dried sorrel with some annoyance. *Oh my God!* The bottle slipped and slid sideways in an effort to break itself. *Have faith, faith. I am catching it.* Her left arm finally wrapped around the gritty lid. Leaning against the wall, she breathed into her center, determined to control this unusual moment.

While all that stupidness was happening, she heard the shop door creak and a melodic baritone call out.

"Kwasi, my man. Ready for the holiday?"

What accent was that? Grenadian? It cut through the air, sugar sweetening sour lemonade. She and the bottle kept leaning against the shelf, savoring the sound of human velvet. Then the bottle slipped again. She juggled.

A soot-black hand held her hand and the bottle still. She followed the long perfectly formed fingers up to see the most strikingly beautiful man. A younger man with startling eye whites, big eyes, long lashes and white teeth. *What the hell was all that eyelash length doing on a man?* It was overwhelming! She sucked her teeth and looked away.

She felt his hand tighten on top of hers and her eyes glazed over. She was sure of it. His midnight black clothes fit him like a glove. *Where did the clothes stop and skin begin? Is he real?* People can see things that are not quite physical.

"Yuh mashing up mi herb shop, June?" Kwasi called out over rustling paper bags.

"Hey Black Cohosh, it's here when you're ready."

She snapped back at Kwasi.

"I thought you said it's not here." She winced at her overly accusatory tone. The man hadn't moved yet. He was too close to her for there to be so much shouting.

"Hmm. No, June," Kwasi laughed. "I'm talking to …. You tell her, Brother."

The velvet man lifted the bottle from June's hand and slipped it back into the empty slot on the alphabetized row. His sleeve pulled tight over his muscled arm. The cuff slipped back, revealing a tattoo of the African Liberation flag. She found her head close to the tattoo. Did his skin make the black in the flag? She put her nose down to his wrist and took a quick sniff. Shocked, she quickly raised herself to look at his knowing eyes.

"Black Cohosh, but you can call me Co." He held out his palm.

As his eyes wandered over her face, June tried to recover. She peeped around him to see if Kwasi had noticed this crazy energy. He had a smile on his face. That herbalist didn't miss a thing. She slowly turned back to the man problem in front of her.

"Hm! You are not making a fool of me today."

"Strange name, right. So it go sometime." Now he was doing the thing with his voice. His baritone flowing over her like baptismal water on a Negril beach, just warm enough. Like that damn cacao and maize soup she had in Grenada five years ago. June hissed her teeth again. This man was making her damn head spin and no man had been allowed to do that in a while.

"Don't mess with me, bwoy." She looked him up and down, secretly trembling as she did. Finally, she turned her palm up to meet his.

Notes

All interior images created in Canva except the items listed below.

The word Caricom in the poem titled "Caricom Cuisine" is an abbreviation for Caribbean Community. It's an intergovernmental organization which comprises twenty member countries, five of whom are associate members. It is the oldest surviving integration movement in the developing world. Its focus includes, trade relations, social and economic justice, maritime interests, and environmental sustainability. https://caricom.org

Photograph for the poem "Somebody Will Come" Associated Press, Publisher. Marcus Garvey. Public domain. Retrieved from Wikimedia Commons <https://commons.wikimedia.org/wiki/File:Marcus_Garvey (1922).jpg>

Photograph for the poem "The Iron On Mi So Bazodee"

Zheyu Huang, Publisher. *Man Wearing a Feather Headdress and Sunglasses.* [Before] Photograph. Retrieved from Unsplash, <https://unsplash.com/photos/a-man-wearing-a-feather-headdress-and-sunglasses-OkkgtaJZ2Yo>.

Photograph for the poem "How was it, Claude?" Bain News Service, Publisher. *Claude McRay i.e. McKay and Baroness v. Freytag i.e. Von Freytag-Loringhoven*. [Before] Photograph. Retrieved from the Library of Congress, <www.loc.gov/item/2014714093/>.

Photograph for the poem "Luminescent Ships"

McCoy, Lauretta. Artist and Publisher. *Luminescent Ships*. Photograph of a painting from the artist's collection.

Photograph for the poem "Questions After a Funeral" Mark A. Johnson, Publisher. Andrea Johnson Ocran. Photograph from Mark A. Johnson's personal collection.

Poem "Games We Dared Not Play With Our Grandmothers." Playground game "Children Children, Yes Mummah" is quoted from the Public Domain. Author and date unknown.

Excerpt in the poem "Dancehall's Unlikely Feminist" General Echo, Riley, Winston. Songwriters. *Arleen*. Single, Techniques Label, 1980.

Acknowledgements

My thanks to Lauretta McCoy for providing human-generated, hand-painted book cover art. To Grace Gordon for providing substantive editing. To Dr. Ezra Engling, Independent Language Consultant, for editing and also for making me understand the critical differences between tonal and phonetic expression. To Vivienne Foster and Ivet Johnson, Caribbean Americans who are lovers of language, stories, and staunch supporters who make sure I get it right. To my family. To Andrene Bonner and Dawn Forrester Price, story mavens and literary kaffeklatch. To Hiram Larew for providing the PoetryXHunger invitations for performance. To the precious purveyors of Caribbean goods and services in the US. To the myriad organizations across the US who provide place as well as cultural and emotional connection on this sojourn in a foreign land. To Aaron Murphy for his effective coaching.

About the Poet

Photo by Yvonne Taylor

Faith P. Nelson is a published poet, freelance copywriter, book developer, and indie publishing consultant. She gained years of experience working behind the scenes at the Embassy of Jamaica in Washington DC, as well as, Black Entertainment Television, a Viacom network. Before that, she was an actress in Jamaica's National Pantomime and other productions. She was also an award-winning soprano under the tutelage of the esteemed musicologist Noel Dexter and Dawn Marie Virtue James. She graduated with a B.A. in English Language and Literature from the University of Maryland, College Park. *Water Therapy* was her first published collection of poetry. Her new chapbook, *Luminescent Ships: Love Songs to Caribbean American Life*, celebrates the diaspora in this region. When not performing poetry, she sings

Caribbean folk music and Reggae in her local area. Faith Nelson's poetry has been published on the *Poetry X Hunger* website, and her poetry has been showcased during *Poetry X Hunger* online poetry readings. Bear, her tabby cat, keeps her company, but runs away when she plays the guitar.

Instagram.com/storydepot

Made in the USA
Middletown, DE
10 May 2025

75239287R00054